ANCHOR BOOKS

SPARE A THOUGHT

Edited by

Heather Killingray

First published in Great Britain in 1998 by
ANCHOR BOOKS
1-2 Wainman Road, Woodston,
Peterborough, PE2 7BU
Telephone (01733) 230761

All Rights Reserved

Copyright Contributors 1998

HB ISBN 1 85930 607 1
SB ISBN 1 85930 602 0

FOREWORD

Anchor Books is a small press, established in 1992, with the aim of promoting readable poetry to as wide an audience as possible.

We hope to establish an outlet for writers of poetry who may have struggled to see their work in print.

The poems presented here have been selected from many entries. Editing proved to be a difficult task and as the Editor, the final selection was mine.

Many poets enjoy the escape of reality that writing a poem allows. It is here that poets can find their inspiration and are able to write down their poetic thoughts and varied emotions.

Spare A Thought is a collection of poetry about many different things, each of which are significant to both the writer and the reader.

This is a collection which is light-hearted and easy to read. It is a suitable poetry book for all.

I trust this selection will delight and please the authors and all those who enjoy reading poetry.

Heather Killingray
Editor

Contents

Winter Sunshine	A J Don	1
The Last Supper	Barbara L Richards	2
A Tiny Seed	Susan Stewart	3
The Seasons	Iris A Carey	4
Just A Thought	Barnaby Newman	5
Two For Me	Kerry Rolfe	6
It's Never Too Late	Geoffrey John Grounds	7
Ghosts	Keith Murdoch	8
Don't Let Me Fall	Kim Montia	9
Breckland Reflections	Jo Ellis	10
Only Love	S J Davidson	11
Children Of The World	Desma P Day	12
Suffer Little Children	Pat Block	13
After The Show - A Child's Song	Richard Stoker	14
The Traveller	Paul Willis	15
The Call	L Jeffries	16
Colours Of The Rain	Clive Weston Sirett	17
Liverpool Rhyme	Lorand Tabith	18
Imagine	Mary Tickle	20
Marriage Of Hearts	Lisa Limb	21
My Body, Soul And Spirit	Jonathan A Sande	22
Untitled	Patricia Fealey	23
Railway Reminiscence	Bakewell Burt	24
A World Of Sound	Tom Clarke	25
Lost	George Ponting	26
Then And Now	D Bird	28
Religion	S C Wiggins	29
Mindhaven-On-Sea	David Pestridge	30
Murder	Don Goodwin	31
Oddfellow	P J Feeney	32
Many Mansions	Monica C Gibson	33
My Day	Ann Beard	34
Retirement	Anne Smith	35
Summer Madness	Betty Thomson	36
Highgate Cemetery	Norah Gordon	37

If Only It Could Be!	Angela Wardell	38
Aspects Of Love	Maureen Watson	39
Happiness	Carole Bloomfield	40
To Dream No More	Kelvin Eagle	41
A Ballad Of The Sea For The One Who I Love	Naomi Snelling	42
Oberon And Tatanin (The Argument)	David Bray	43
Escalation Thro' Frustration!	Hilary Jill Robson	44
Summertime	Liam Lewis	46
A Tribute To My Nephew	Keena	47
Time To Change	Daisy Cooper	48
The Omen	Moor 'Ender	49
Maylord Orchards - It's Primordial Peace	Rev S E F Sheppard	50
The Day I Drank Champagne For Breakfast	Brenda Pritchard	52
Heroes Of The Skies	Margaret Howens	53
The Sand Lovers	Joyce Barry	54
My Shell	Katie O'Brien	56
Unwanted Memory	Christine Nicholson	57
My Heart Is Yours	Doreen Margaret Sirett	58
Country Scene	GIG	59
The Soldier On The Battlefield	Stephen Hunt	60
Road Rage	James Hodgson	62
Behind Closed Doors	Adela Llewellyn	63
Precious	Victoria Sutton	64
We Can Only Do So Much	Jean Beardsmore	65
Geoff Hemming Is The Afternoon Man	Coleen Bradshaw	66
The Boy Who Steals Hearts	Michelle J Cartwright	67
Who?	Peter Evans	68
On Behalf Of Them	T M Welbourne	69
Man Among Polluted Stars	David Hazlett	70
Bircham River-Bed Sunset	Katherine Latham Grimes	71
Mother	D Burke	72
Just Another Day	Saheeda Khan	73
A Night To Remember	Jennifer Polledri	74

It Shows In Your Face	William Price	76
Bath Time For The Dog	Wendy Watkin	77
The Same Language	Paul Beretta	78
The Way I Wish	Alan Green	80
Season Of Life	Michael Chappell	81
Dumb Animals	Phyllis O'Connell	82
Alone	Tammy Louise Gayle Tiffany	84
Love Came Without Warning	Betty Mealand	85
The Greed To Have	Jim Sargant	86
My Garden	Mary Welsh	88
Believe	Patricia McDonald	89
Candlelit Dinner	B Page	90
If Only	Elizabeth Bulleyment	91
To The New-Born Child	Christine Osborne	92
Love	George	93
The Wedding	James S Jarvis	94
Incompatible	Joy Sanders	95
For You	Julie White	96
Pain	Warren Brown	97
Your Eyes	Wendy Smith	98
Angel Of The North	Margaret Wallis	99
Tina My Daughter	Albert Moses	100
The Sands Of Time	Gail Susan Halstead	101
Hands That Feed	Dorothy Grey	102
April Evening	Jessie F Harper	103
Swan Song	Ivy Cawood	104
The Supporter	Roy Lewis	105
Keith	David Tallach	106
Rust	Robert D Shooter	107
To An For Our Beloved Country	Jim Hacobian	108
Upward . . .	Gordon Long	109
A Photograph	Hugh Jackson	110
Agony Aunt	T Burke	111
Evening	J C Atkinson	112
Pilgrimage	Sheila Manley	113
Passchendaele (Ypres 1917)	Michele Collatina	114
The Traveller's Faith	Ty Allbright	116
Mother	May Kay	117

WINTER SUNSHINE

The New Year trod a footstep through the door
with blasting winds and swirling snowflakes white
until in utter silence came the thaw,
an end to winter's agonising bite;

In quiet solitude I list' and saw
the joyous fledglings on the wing take flight
to where the sunshine gleamed across the moor
and where the meadow buttercups were bright;

So like a kitten with a playful paw
I grasped the flick'ring sunshine with delight,
a golden autumn I could not ignore,
I lingered still and ev'rything seemed right;
the firelight tossed the seasons all around
when blizzards swept the New Year's frozen ground.

A J Don

THE LAST SUPPER

The food arrived, but no-one cared
Wine flowed to fill each waiting cup
The table groaned in self-defence
The condemned man said, 'Bottoms up!'
Unleavened bread sat on a dish
Its sell-by date said 'nice and fresh'
The man broke this and gave each guest
a piece and said, 'This is my flesh'
'It still tastes like bread' muttered one to himself
but the man overheard. 'It's a metaphor, you ass!'
'This wine is my blood . . . use your imagination'
The guest kept his head down and let that one pass.
Soon, the last meal was over
The man drained his cup,
tasted dregs of eternity a second too long
and said with a sigh, 'OK, who's washing up?'
To the guest whose head remained guiltily bowed
he said, 'Where there's muck there's money, I believe . . .
In a potter's field we will bury this cup -
it'll be rarer than rocking-horse poo one day . . . you'll see'

Barbara L Richards

A TINY SEED

Plant a tiny seed with love
And watch it grow
Each day a little more
It stretches up towards the sky
With outstretched arms it seems to fly.

Branching outwards as it goes
Buds appearing
Then the leaves
How they quiver in the breeze.

Sun is shining all aglow
Fruit is forming what a show
Berries ripe the tree's alive
Different species of birds arrive.

The north wind blows
A robin twitters
And how the little bird it shivers
The snow glitters all around
And peace and quiet and love abound.

Susan Stewart

THE SEASONS
*(To my dear friend Maureen who was a young
land army girl before she went to live in Australia)*

How the winter frost does glow,
Bringing forth the shimmering snow.
Soon spring will be here,
Bringing pink blossom on the bough,
Soon to come the summer too.
Hot sun and colours of flowers blooming.
When we find autumn brings
Brown and golden leaves that fall
Then but once again to find winter around
Bringing Christmas with message clear -
Oh how soon that was this year . . .

Iris A Carey

JUST A THOUGHT

I don't claim to know it all
I don't even do my bit
I just sit upon that wall
Like every other hypocrite
Who says the world's still spinning round
What's the problem, what's the rush?
It won't happen in our lifetime
Everyone worries too much.

We will carry on destroying
All the wars will still be fought
And I'm sorry for suggesting
Any of us could be taught
It was only just a thought

Barnaby Newman

TWO FOR ME

A cup of coffee
A mug of tea
A spoon of sugar
  two for me
A chocolate biscuit
A lump of cake
A round jam doughnut
  on my plate.
Banoffee pie
the cream piled high
Treacle pudding
yellow custard running
Jelly and ice cream
one scoop or two
A cup of coffee
A mug of tea
A spoon of sugar
  two for me!

Kerry Rolfe

IT'S NEVER TOO LATE

The needle so sharp like the grip in my hand
I need council - oh council, weird thoughts that surround.
There's dots on my skin and jabs that command
Serving like lessons, till my turn comes round.

The air is so heavy, also quite thick
The reaching and pain, it's really quite sick.
My thoughts are drowning with pleas of despair.
The castles I dreamt of like dust in the air.

Pulses race, convulsions are quick
Faces of fear seem grim and bewitched.
Lips that mime the words not there
A sweat-filled body I don't care, I don't care.

There's a hand on my shoulder
With a beckoning smile
Please God no, please God no,
Just a while, just a while.

On youthful face 'twas plain to see
The mask of death did'st settle on me.
So sit up, take notice and let it sink in
It's not gear or gas, that makes it a sin.

The world is round we've proven all that
It's people within so why can't it last.
Yesterday's honour, tomorrow's crime
The tale is told, the sorrow all mine.

Geoffrey John Grounds

GHOSTS

What would you do
on a hot windless night
in an empty house
if you heard a door bang?

Go and investigate?
Snuggle under the sheet?
Believe in an explanation?
Or believe in ghosts?

Keith Murdoch

DON'T LET ME FALL

Don't let me fall, please
Hold me tight
Don't sacrifice me
To the night

Ignore the silver
Of the moon
The wolves are singing out
Their tune

My back is bare
Lend me your coat
Remove the chain
About my throat

Protect me from
Those unseen eyes
Those whispered voices
And their lies

Help guide me through
The tangled trees
And mountain pathways
No-one sees

Give me the strength
To carry on
Stay by my side
'Til night has gone

Kim Montia

BRECKLAND REFLECTIONS

Leaden skies, and a biting wind
    Sends snowflakes drifting in the square.
Late shoppers, heads bent against the chilling air,
    Hurry homeward, and glad to be going there.

Noisy starlings squabble for their nightly perch
    Having spent the total day in on-going search for food
Greedily eating everything in sight,
    Depriving tits and robins of their special treat.

Wild geese call harshly as they fly overhead
    Returning to nearby reeds, in which to make their bed.
Behind the plough, hungry seagulls bank and wheel,
    Calling loudly, as they swoop to snatch one last meal.

Soon a blanket of snow will cover the breckland.
    The forest trees, already tipped in white
Give shelter to the gentle hind.
    No artist's canvas can capture God's peace
        in such a sight.

Jo Ellis

ONLY LOVE

Just for you dear wife,
Does this very special memorandum come
With the fastest of speed,
Conveying with them true thoughts of love

Yes, we've shared a tear or more
Along with happy times too, with great thralldom
Our thoughts were together in auspices
And sometimes I never saw the light

That was so affably pointed out,
By the love of my life of many years,
For this I accept my wrong doing
And ask only for forgiveness,

And maybe, stored in our hearts,
Will we come to life's full terms,
When any problems arise are shared
Will an inspiration be in sight

But then, its only left to our regulation
In the best way that we see,
And which ever way we choose to go,
I know, it will have been done conjointly

For this dear wife of mine,
I can only say a great thank you,
In putting up with everyday problems experienced
In a solid kind of way that love means

S J Davidson

CHILDREN OF THE WORLD

Children, little children everywhere
Homeless, hungry, just stand and stare.
Homes and parents lost through war
Devastation and deprivation is more and more.
Children do not go to school
No facilities, so it's not the rule.
Contaminated water and little food
Staving children, many in the nude.
With sewerage running down the street
And many flies buzz in the heat.
No toys or grassy place to play,
All very sad and never gay.
Many children maimed by land mines,
Put in the ground by thoughtless swines.
Can we help these destitute folk?
Their living conditions is no joke.
Princess Di was doing so much
Helping people by her touch.
Let us then try to improve
And all these ghastly things remove.
So much misery everywhere,
Albania, Bosnia and Zaire
Not forgetting India, Ethiopia and Peru
These are some - to name a few.
Little children, we think of you
And wish there was more that we could do.

Desma P Day

SUFFER LITTLE CHILDREN

Lots of little children
in this world today,
Don't know love or kindness,
Don't have enough food,
Warm clothes, things they
        really *need,*
All because the world
  is full of hate and
        greed.
They are God's children
   They are children
       in *need.*

Pat Block

AFTER THE SHOW - A CHILD'S SONG

Long after all have gone
upon a deserted dusty stage
where three months past a show was staged
I come upon an old piano
brown and long
against the wall in window light it stands
as no-one's there I make this sound
and reaching up my head and hands I see
trees and pavements black and white
a sort of draughts
my fingers walk upon them in the centre where it's bright
now when I explore
with fingertips and step that's sure
I find the darkest farthest ends
are fun to reach with thumb and finger
here my friends galore
sing and dance with me this song
fairies at top and giants below and
if I stretch out further the fairies sing
the giants shout together
and coming closer
elves and gnomes and pixies battle for its sunny centre
now when all is done
my friends return to the farthest ends
of my old piano
to two brown stones where they must live
for once behind a chair I hid
and watched a man dust them away but they
returned to sing and play
the next day!

Richard Stoker

THE TRAVELLER

Small stones beneath his feet
Grind on smaller stones,
The traveller stops and steadies himself,
His boots grip and keep him from sliding.
Closing his eyes he tilts his head backwards,
The cool drink from his canteen refreshes him.
Before stopping
He had felt no reality for time or distance.
His steps had merged together
Like the clouds merging above him.
Now, looking back, he can see
Just how far he has come.
Looking forward, he can see,
Just how far he has left to go.
When he had started climbing
He had felt like giving up, but now,
Now he felt encouraged, and far more determined.

Paul Willis

THE CALL

Five fingers on the pulse of life,
each with its own selective role.
One felt the warmth of something young,
the chill of something old.
One smelt the freshness of the spring
and, too, the dying rose.
One saw the mornings fresh and clear,
the evenings soft and gentle.
One tasted all the fruits of life:
the cool: the sentimental.
One heard the high notes of the lark,
the low notes of the chapel bell,
the whispered tenderness of love,
the violent moments that were hell,
and then it heard the call!
I was afraid and wrapped my fingers
'round my weak and feeble frame,
protesting I was much too young,
protesting I was feeble, maimed,
protesting that this hand of mine
was made to honour and fulfil,
but no . . . no not to kill!
And then again there came the call!
Oh life, so dull yet precious now!
Oh feeble heart, why thump so fast?
Don't kill me while protesting how
I'm much too young to die . . .
but high above my crumbling wall
there comes again the call!
Five fingers that five senses were
reached out to seek the truth,
and out of all the truth they found
the wondrous lie that stole our youth.

L Jeffries

COLOURS OF THE RAIN

Coming suddenly
out of the woods
On the side of a hill,
I wiped the rain from
my eyes,
The earth . . .
was running free,
With a warm trickling
brightness.

Hailstones and rainbows,
Everywhere the grass grows,
beneath
White scuds of thorn trees
Lit . . .
by straight shafts
of light
from a thunder crack
in the dark sky,
On this wild April day.

Clive Weston Sirett

LIVERPOOL RHYME

Diana, Diana,
Immortalised
A legend, a legend
Love sweetly rhyme

Football the name
Football we play
Football the game
Football the great

Legends of yesterday
Legends today
Football a legend
Football the game

National sport
National event
Nation's own sweetheart
Nation's own legends

The Queen of Hollywood
A Yankee Dame
Marilyn Monroe
A legend but never the same

For the very first time
History is to immortalise
The Queen of Hearts
On a gun carriage
Lay the legend of love

A tribute to love
The nation's own love

Love is forever
Love the Liverpool rhyme
Football is the nation's
Love
National pastime

Black ink poetry
Written in black
For the sake of sweet love

Lorand Tabith

IMAGINE

If we could swing amongst the clouds
We'd gather all the blue
and put in just a touch of sun
to make a marvellous hue
We'd gather all the glittering stars
and much to our delight
we'd find a way to stop the dark
descending every night
We'd build a stairway to the stars
and line it all with gold
we'd paint the clouds with sunshine
such wonders to behold

Mary Tickle

MARRIAGE OF HEARTS

I believe in a marriage of hearts.
But this is more like a horse and cart.
Our rings and certificate of paper,
Was just to make you feel safer.

A big ego-trip it was for you,
Showing the world a new good you.
But soon to be staying away too long,
Leaving like a stranger soon after dawn.

This marriage is starting to starve,
All I wanted was a good laugh.
Being real stupid and totally daft,
Now my heart's shipwrecked on a raft.

Desperate, lonely and in need,
A heart yearning to be free.
You turned our paradise to ice,
Another unlucky throw of the dice.

I wish I could make you suffer,
But the fault is your father and mother's.
Estranged and left out on a limb,
Allowed to wallow in your whims.

Your past is ruining your future,
Can't fight off the bottle's allure.
The demons dance at your failure,
You've rejected love as your saviour.

Lisa Limb

MY BODY, SOUL AND SPIRIT

My body is only fresh,
And too soft as a sponge,
That will crumble,
Once I die.
My soul which is, as
Strong as an iron sword,
Has never gone into despair,
Or even let me down,
When I think of death, and
My spirit which is, as
Solid as a mountain rock,
Will always live forever after,
In my absence,
For more and more,
Million years to come.

Jonathan A Sande

UNTITLED

Sultry kisses with this rose,
To warm your nights thru' winter snows,
Each little swirling crystal flake
Cools your body from the love we make,
Searching, touching, love me, love me,
Petals from the rose above me . . .

Patricia Fealey

RAILWAY REMINISCENCE

Railings and boundary fences
Are all that remain intact,
Deserted tunnels and lonely bridges,
Keep watch over the silent track.

The future, remains as only a memory,
Of that which once had been,
Slowly drawing the final curtain,
On a stage no longer with a scene.

What more could anyone ever wish for,
- As a tribute -
To the mile upon mile of railway graveyard,
Than 'nature' - as the curator,
The lines' very own final guard.

Waving from the embankments,
Flags - not only of red and green,
- But of a thousand different colours -
A fitting and poignant reminder,
- Of the age -
When the railways reigned supreme.

Bakewell Burt

A WORLD OF SOUND

Only seagulls and curlews sing
when in the air and on the wing.
Snowflakes dance about all day
when sunshine has then flown away.
Daffodils trumpet a happy call,
on green stems they do grow so tall
and in the woodlands you can hear,
the bluebells ringing soft but clear.
Berries which are very red
are munched by sparrows
the farmer said.
Thunder from the clouds above,
fills all the sky with fear not love.
Autumn leaves fall to the ground
and make a brittle crunchy sound.
When stars peep out
and darkness comes,
then quickly to my home I run.
I slam the door and turn the key
and calm my nerves with pots of tea.
The heart keeps bumping through the night.
My sweetheart has now gone from sight.
When all alone and feeling low,
I pray to make the spirit grow.

Tom Clarke

Lost

I was lost in deep
despair,
I looked to heaven,
I saw you there;
In my loneliness you
took my hands,
In my darkest hour,
you brought the sun;
When I was lost,
showed me the way;
Turned my 'swamp' of
sorrows to golden sands;
You are my dreams of
far-off lands;
You saved my life;
Made my 'heaven on earth';
My 'paradise':
You are the angel that
guards my soul;
You gave me comfort, you
Gave me peace;
When I was sad, you gave
a kiss,
When I was cold, you kept
me warm,
As I cried, you gave me
love,
No greater gift from heaven
was this:
You gave me strength to
carry on my chosen 'role';

Gave me your heart, gave me
your soul:
But most of all;
Gave me your love.

George Ponting

THEN AND NOW

Learner of trades not study or desk,
Lover of beer, wine, friendship and jest.
Lover of women, love of kids
Fighting his way to the manhood he craves
Man for the people, his self is ignored
He picks up the pieces of burning, of gore
Strength is his virtue, strength of the mind
Strength that maintains them and withstands the grime
Man with a purpose, man with a goal
Man with a life, life's insanity stole.

Locked in his cell, he surveys the wreckage,
Of the man he once was, a strange kind of homage.
Built over years, destroyed in an instant
Destroyed in insanity hard to imagine
Suicidal destruction, built up in despair
Dressed in boozed-up stupidity, mind starved of air.

Now bereft of his freedom, his future returns
The dreams of the boy, the love that he yearns
Surrounded by love, the child once again
Abides in the man and his strength is regained.
Strength for his family fills him with pride
The strength of a woman, their son by his side
No longer his soul soaked in drink and despair
Mind flooded with oxygen, bubbling with air
What matter these locks and bars made of steel
Captivity can't take what the heart and mind feel.
Can't take the completeness
Can't take the joy
Can't take the euphoria
Of loving mother and boy.

D Bird

Religion

I have always said of God, that I do not believe
For to believe in what one cannot see, I just cannot perceive
And looking round the world today, at every troubled land
With war and hate and suffering, it is hard to understand
For if we are God's children, and He our Father be
Why does He not control us, is the thing that bothers me
When children are still suffering, while their parents fight
If God so loves His children, then how can this be right
There is so much of religion, I have never understood
Even if I read the Bible, I still don't think I would
For is it fact or fiction, how can one be sure
And if written all those years ago, is it relevant anymore
This is just my opinion, as it has been all along
So if we should meet in Heaven, then I will know that I was wrong.

S C Wiggins

MINDHAVEN-ON-SEA

Let me tell you of a little haven I know, which I visit nearly every day,
A secluded sanctuary by the sea, my private little bay.
Never do human feet tread upon its shores, but for those that carry me there,
Never do human eyes gaze upon its tides, but for my own very privileged pair.
And I've even put a chair there, a photographer would place his tripod in that spot,
And to the left is a little table, with tea brewing in a china teapot.
I love to gaze at the blue sea and blue sky, broken only by the whiteness of the gull,
Just like the cup of tea in my hand, I've serenity's measure to the full.
And sometimes when it's lashed by rain and high winds, I go to visit my secret cove,
In the exquisite shelter of my little caravan, I'll await the kettle on the stove.
This bay can be whatever I make it, I need not seek for I always find,
For this sumptuous little slice of heaven, is a haven of my mind.
I can steer my mind's eye from its frenzied state, and jump into a big escape hole,
Whenever the stresses and stains of this life, weight heavily upon my soul.
In seconds I'm at peace in another world, a place that anxiety can't touch,
When used in a positive way such as this, the imagination's such a powerful crutch.
So, dear reader of my poem, create a beautiful haven of your mind,
A secluded place to which you can go, where you leave unwanted baggage behind.
When in an anxious situation, others may wonder why you don't overwind,
You'll smile because you know what they don't know, about the haven in your mind.

David Pestridge

MURDER

There's been another murder in our town.
Seems that morals and standards are going down.
Children don't know who their fathers are.
They've got to have a brand new car.
They are a product of all this free love.
God knows it's wrong. Why heaven's above.
Years ago few got divorced I know.
In two parent families most did grow.
Now single parent families are the norm.
Poor little kids out of wedlock now born.
With no role models in their lives.
They should have parents, a man and wife.

Don Goodwin

ODDFELLOW

He wandered past so many times, his heart so sick and bare,
O'er road and rail and path he went and no-one knew to care,
Sometimes he stopped, but not for long, a stranger wouldn't dare,
To see anew, to ponder too, to wonder who lived there.

He oft' heard laughter from within, but could not see a face,
Imagined all the sweetest things, that must by right take place,
Imagined one was fair and slim and she with turned-up nose,
A child in blue, or maybe two, a love sublime, who knows?

He oft' saw toys upon a lawn, in need of slight repair,
And lines by day where billowed clothes, washed with love and care,
Seen happy chimneys belching smoke, that told of warmth within,
And sometimes 'man's best friend' came out, to poke around the bin.

With collar raised agin the cold, tense arms in pockets deep,
He wandered on into the night and sometimes he did weep,
He wept for those he just passed by, asked him above to keep,
The love, that often fragile thing, safe, secure whilst asleep.

P J Feeney

MANY MANSIONS

My heart is full of sadness,
I love you so my own,
I'll walk along my head held high,
And journey on alone.

I'll do the things you wish me to,
And smile, although I'm sad,
I know you're waiting for me,
A thought that makes me glad.

In our Father's house I know,
Are many mansions high,
And you'll prepare a place for me,
Up in that bright, blue sky.

We've walked through life together,
It's up and downs we've trod,
Together we have harmonised,
The rules set out by God.

Monica C Gibson

My Day

Just drifting in the stillness,
Of the early morning air.
A sense of calm and tranquillity,
Moments one can't compare!

Sounds of movement is sensed,
Waiting for that moment in time.
For every new day is different,
An excitement one can't define!

Then suddenly the sun rises,
And the world has come alive.
With the buzzing of the traffic,
For man's fighting to survive!

As the sun gathers strength,
Its warmth filters through.
But we take this for granted,
Life's hectic with too much to do!

Drifting back to my place of rest,
It's time for the sun to go down.
The darkness is now gathering,
Again calm and tranquillity is found!

Ann Beard

RETIREMENT

I live a very busy life,
I thank God that I can.
When I retired from teaching
Is when my life began.
I thought I'd take it easy
After twenty years in school,
But I really was mistaken
My friends thought me a fool,
Because I started growing plants
To sell for charity,
My greenhouse wasn't big enough
So that was not to be.
I started writing poetry
I thought I had a gift,
My friends enjoyed the verse I wrote
So that gave me a lift.
And then I joined the local church
I needed something more,
I didn't know until this year
Just what would be in store.
I'm now the church's treasurer,
A most important post,
Of all the things which interest me
I like this job the most.

Anne Smith

SUMMER MADNESS

Steep as a mountain, high as a cloud,
The river close by and yet not a sound,
Why do you buy such a place they all say,
As they walk down the path at the end of the day
You are not getting younger they all repeat,
As they reach the bottom and sit on the seat.

I need to provide myself with a choice,
With birds and bees and an echoing voice,
For those who want houses, shops and a street,
Don't buy a place all peaceful and neat
You can have buses, aeroplanes too
But I want a garden all fresh with dew
So let's all be thankful at the end of the day
Whatever we have we all can say
As the sun sets and you all go home
I've the birds and the bees, so I'm never alone.

Betty Thomson

HIGHGATE CEMETERY

Only the dead lie silent
While high in treetops owls communicate
With shrieks of night-time mysteries
And in the undergrowth below
The foxes make their noises
Like fighting cats recalling conquests
And birds they tore to pieces
In wilder days.

Then when the night is over
The birds take charge again
Singing their sweeter songs
To greet the living
With hopes of new tomorrows
But still the dead lie silent.

Norah Gordon

IF ONLY IT COULD BE!

Why is there killing
Slaughtering of innocent people
Adults murdered by adults
Children slayed by children
What happened to loving one another
We barely hear the words love and compassion
Now over-ridden by hatred and violence
Are we to hope that this will end

When will we stop injecting our children's minds with graphical
scenes of torture and bloodshed,
Portraying these to be the norm
Is it not hypocrisy to teach them right from wrong,
Then to subject them to slaughter
Can there be hope in a world wrought with evil
Can there be an end to hatred, violence and killing

Can there be an explosion of love, compassion and well-being,
To rock the very foundations of humanity,
Pouring into every well
Then completed,
Joined together to form a united peaceful world
Oh if only it could be!

Angela Wardell

ASPECTS OF LOVE

The verb to love - so many implications,
and fascination
in translation.

Heartfelt, deep, no reservations,
full emotion
with devotion.

Passion, heady, intoxication,
captivation
just fascination.

Love to help - illustration,
a demonstration,
explanation?

See an item - appreciation,
adoration
mesmerisation.

Friendship, happy invitations,
close relations
fraternisation.

The verb to love - so many implications,
and fascination
in translation.

Maureen Watson

HAPPINESS

Happiness is a brief moment in time
in a world that's full of filth and grime.
Happiness is a blink of the eyes
in a world full of perversions and lies.
Happiness is the real gift of life
in a world full of evil and strife.
Happiness is a word full of meaning
in a world that needs a thorough cleaning.
Let's get rid of cruelty, violence and hate
and open the door and begin a new slate.

Carole Bloomfield

TO DREAM NO MORE

Is today the day I've waited for?
I'm trapped inside my private world.
I'm waiting to cross my bridge of dreams,
Hoping that tomorrow brings the beginning for
My world of dreams.
To change the future, to dream no more.
Is this the day I've waited for, is this the day?
This dream I fear is not unique, for many of us sit and think.
We think the thoughts that make the dreams,
Hoping that tomorrow brings the beginning for our world of dreams.
As time drifts on with my dreams withheld,
I change those dreams to suit my world.
For today my dreams have been and gone,
They're locked away, they're safe and unused.
They're absorbing time, they're looking on, to create a future.
For my world of dream, for my world of dreams.

Kelvin Eagle

A Ballad Of The Sea For The One Who I Love

Come, dance with me the shores of sand,
Let rhythm rock the sky-spilled seas,
Let living be an active verb,
Come, hold my hand and breathe.

Come, my love, laugh at the lonely,
Smash night with every atom moving
Treading, rising, falling shadows
Sharing soft, let's tide with ease.

My deepest loved one, wave the waves
Drive every burning diminuendo,
Close your eyes, let's waltz abandon,
Circling through the trembling years.

Naomi Snelling

OBERON AND TATANIN (THE ARGUMENT)

Within a little elfin grot
the fairy King there stood
and facing lovely Tatania
who in temper wild with reddened cheek
the fairy Queen with fiery eyes fierce words did speak
and thus pursued the argument
now it is said that rage will quell
within the heart where love does dwell
but whether or not this was to be
is part of fairy history.

David Bray

ESCALATION THRO' FRUSTRATION!

Refused to attend school to take the exam;
Fifteen years and tall; thought himself a man!
She could not use force or take him by the hand
Nor lead him with reins, nor bridle noseband.
                        'Who would be a mum?'

She begged, coaxed, ranted and sent the rebel off,
He returned via the rear; declined to back off,
Hot-footed to his room, a family outlaw,
Locked himself in; pushed wardrobe against door.
                        'Now what?'

Exams had commenced; far too late to persist,
Time, silence, elapsed! - He'd not cut his wrist?
The more she pondered the greater she worried;
What was he doing? She became flurried.
                        'He surely wouldn't!'

Underneath his window she placed a ladder,
Gingerly climbed; with each step becoming madder,
Peeped over the sill he sat in the 'robe,
Knees clasped before him as a xenophobe.
                        'Whatever is he doing?'

Incredulous disbelief! They exchanged stares,
And - she atop a ladder, not top of the stairs!
Ordered, 'Open the window to let me in!'
Ignored! She found she was no heroine!
                        'I'm stuck up here!'

Her legs turned to jelly, she quivered and cried,
She'd overlooked heights she could not abide.
A friend arrived, 'What are you doing up there?
Oh! You're up the ladder, in the 'robe's your heir!'
                        'I've been transfixed half an hour!'

'What do you mean you cannot move? Quickly!
Pull yourself together!' she said, intently.
'Waiting for your coffin or a fire engine?
Rung by rung, you'll be fine once you begin!'
        'I cannot move!'

Gripping spokes tightly she gradually descended,
Arrived at base upright not upended,
Standing sure-footedly upon terra firma,
'Maybe next year's exams,' she did murmur.
       'What have I done to deserve this?'

In frustration, relief, fell upon the bed,
What she thought about son best left unsaid;
Next day he said 'Must take one day at a time,
If I've made a mistake the fault is mine!'
'Sorry Mum!'

Hilary Jill Robson

SUMMERTIME

Summer has come, it's time for heat,
Under the trees, the shade you will meet.
Many days you will see no rain,
Many people look at the skies in vain,
Every day the sun gets hotter,
Red sunburnt people drink litres of water.

The heat is too hot, people wish it was winter,
It makes people overreact, if they are hurt by a splinter,
Many hot days, will soon be over,
Everyone goes on holiday, for instance, say Dover.

Liam Lewis

A Tribute To My Nephew

He was a loving caring lad
He never caused a scene
He made his parents very proud
To know that he wasn't mean.

He always took his mum
Out on a shopping spree
He always bought gifts for
His friends and family.

He enjoyed going for a drink
With his dad at the weekend
They would play at snooker
Laugh and joke his dad
Was like a friend.

He always was the best man
At friends' weddings he went to
He was a snazzy dancer
He would dance the whole night through.

He was a smartly dressed man
He looked good enough to eat
He was the kind of guy, that made
You proud if he met you in the street.

He always went on holiday with
His friend and his two brothers
But the best friends he had
Were a loving dad and a very loving mother.

Keena

TIME TO CHANGE

Where are the nappies, that danced on the line
Cut from an old sheet, that was weathered with time
They danced all night, they danced all day
Till they too were worn away.

Then came Terry's a luxury for bums
A brand new range for all those mums
Soaked at night with a brisk little boil
In mam's gas boiler, where nothing would spoil.

Along came the washer, a nappy's delight
No more soaking throughout the night
Packed like herrings in a tin
Oh what a chuckle, when they started to spin.

Gone are the Terry's they had their day
Pampers here are they to stay
The wheelie bin is worried in stress
Where can I put this horrible mess.

Mother Earth is grumbling too
With all these Pampers what can she do
Now all her tips of coming alive
With all this food, they sure do thrive.

Pampers too, may have had their day
Tomorrow they will have found a way
Just something for those little bums
And help those tired old working mums.

At the end of the day, with no way out
Surely you can find an old sheet about
Cut into squares, not costing a dime
Do we move on, or go back in time?

Daisy Cooper

THE OMEN

I am a black and shiny crow
You humans are my only foe

From pole to pole I've colonised
By every race and creed despised

But, me and mine we'll sit and wait
On chimney pot and farmer's gate

Until you've blown yourselves apart
In silly war games that you start

And then from some dark quarried hole
Or vault or cave from pole to pole

I'll colonise it one more time
And your world then will all be mine

Moor 'Ender

MAYLORD ORCHARDS - IT'S PRIMORDIAL PEACE
((A Hereford city centre shopping street, long pedestrianized, its history lost in the mists of time))

Maylord Orchards, Elysian Field
Where trees, long gone their fruits they'd yield -
Pears and plums, and figs so ripe:
Fig-leaf to cover the gender's type . . .
Apples for 'coider' rolled by the stone
Giant-sized, once turned by mule alone.
Trees there famed for fertility,
Fertilised anew. In their lee
Shady nooks and paths we see,
Laid aeons ago for perpetuity.
So - let us walk, holding hands awhile
Midst traffic's noise 'magined, in singles' file,
For, of a nobler past that wanes -
Replacing e'en cars, their still sombre lanes . . .

Return us then to happier times -
Olives or dates paired, marrying lines!
Trees to climb - oaks, ash and birch,
Children up high on branches to perch;
Boughs to carve your initials in,
Using pen-knives or bits of tin;
Branches to make love underneath,
Twigs of mistletoe, holly for the wreath.
With burials beneath - 'twas custom of yore,
Deity's Blessing on His Dead to pour.

Two knights-of-old engaged in duel
In some clearing in this orchard cool:
Since - felled for timber or firewood,
Can we picture those trees, planted - for food,
Of fruits and nuts and all things good?
Now dead! In solemn stands these stood,
Whence, we disperse, trek to our homes,
Leaving memory's orchards, defunct alone . . .

S E F Sheppard

THE DAY I DRANK CHAMPAGNE FOR BREAKFAST

I drank champagne for breakfast by crystal waters blue,
Soaking up the noon day sun I've now had quite a few,
I do believe I'm tipsy, my head is in a spin,
I cannot understand it I'm not like this on gin.
Shall I go and skinny dip and shock all those about,
By peeling off my cossie and let it all hang out.
Well I've been and gone and done it, the first time I must say,
I'm having such a good time here in this pool today.
I flirted with a nice young man who looked like some Greek god,
And just like me and with a wink his clothes he too did shod.
I asked him if he'd like a drink, of my champagne it's good,
It didn't take him long to think, I really knew he would.
Champagne's now gone right to my head, and with lust in mind
                                                                        we went to bed,
'Geronimo' was shouted as he swung from chandelier,
And with only just his socks on he did look rather queer.
We spent a night of passion in hotel room 101,
And unbeknown to both of us I did conceive a son,
Now my drinking days are over, I knew they could not last,
And I'll not forget that special day I drank champagne for breakfast.

Brenda Pritchard

HEROES OF THE SKIES

From strife stricken lands and plains
Heading homewards comes the planes
Flaring bombers of fighting fame
Limps towards home through the skies
Pray! Hope and faith have its care
'Cause of the fighter pilot's nightmare
Bravely sounds of prayer the crew share
Such great courage is in risk
As suddenly the place becomes hit!
Yet onwards goes the war hit plane
On forwards o'er a briny brink
Ah! Vast and deep this threatening jinx
O far below the mighty ocean beckoned
Still heroes of the skies with faces blackened
E'er always had one thought in mind
Oh! Keep the bomber a-flying high
Ne'er discard it upon the waves
Let's get our plane safely back to base
Indeed all such brave heroes together
A great team who shall stay forever
Heroes of the skies
E'en long after the team crew disbands
E'er forever some bomber fortress
Remains ever and ever some keepsake upon land.

Margaret Howens

THE SAND LOVERS

A blooming hot sun in Croydon
Dad's black motorcycle combination
A glossy hussy, waxed and polished
Built for speed, good looks and British
Fuelled for adventure, gallons of thrill
Calls, toot-tooting, chaotic packing finished
Revs gently rocking, scattering dust
Pulls away with powerful thrust
Ramsgate, hotter than the Sahara desert.

Sandwiches, pickle, apples and pear
All together in a big brown bag
Four vibrant rugs, one for each
Bucket and spade, maggots, rod.
Blankets, ground sheet, Primas stove
With goldfish making such a fuss
Slopping cold water all over us
We have a dog, he couldn't come
Poor old chap, he's being done
Totally brill when we finally move
Fruity beauty, humming in her prime
Hugging the road ahead, with the best.

Hot sand, ice cream and lemonade,
Summer, easy for Mum to say 'Yes.'
To dream on green grass under stars
Really appealed to our adventurousness
Breeze smelling strongly of sea
Had us snoring, asleep in a trice
Eggs and bacon at the small café
Morning would see us browning, nice.

Hot sand running between the toes
Hunting the pool for shell and crab
Dad would be gone, seemed like hours
Basking, like a whale, face to the sun
Back he'd come happy and young.

Joyce Barry

My Shell

Clasped close, to my ear,
I hear the sea.
Windy lullaby, clear,
Soothes the child in me.

Tight shut my eyes,
I dream I'm there.
Rolling waves crescendo,
Drown reality,
Through salt stung air.

My heart races,
It rises with the tide.
Toes curled in sinking, wet sand -
Stretching far to the glistening line,
Revealing damp, desert land.

Dancing,
Making pictures with my tracks.
I am hunting for unusual stones.
So, so happy beneath the rocks.
Here my spirit is at home.

Katie O'Brien

UNWANTED MEMORY

I catch a glimpse of the past,
So long ago yet so near.
The memory comes so fast
Covering my thoughts with fear.

So long ago yet so near
Why did I not leave it behind?
Covering my thoughts with fear,
I sit back to watch my mind.

Why did I not leave it behind?
The power was given by you.
I sit back to watch my mind
At its mercy I see it through.

The power was given by you,
The scars will never fade.
At its mercy I see it through,
I am closer to whom this has made.

The scars will never fade.
The memory comes so fast,
I am closer to whom this has made,
I catch a glimpse of the past.

Christine Nicholson

MY HEART IS YOURS

I have lost you . . .
Will I ever see you again?
The breath that I breathe
Belongs to you . . .
Your love lit up my soul,
Pearly - white teeth
Skin so fresh.

You are my inspiration,
My love is like a flower
In a field of green grass,
Wild poppies dancing
On a light breeze.
You are the petal
I am the thorn . . .
Come back to me!

Doreen Margaret Sirett

COUNTRY SCENE

Gentle are most raindrops
Falling to the ground
Silent are the snowflakes
That fall without a sound.
A breeze is sighing softly
As it rustles through the trees
Falling like confetti
A kaleidoscope of leaves.
Moonlight shadows quietly fade
As appears a misty dawn
Silver cobwebs in the haze
Lie on a bed of thorns.
Wisps of cloud, float on by
To reveal a thread of blue
The sun begins to climb on high
And kiss the morning dew.
Daffodils and daisies, dance in a meadow green
A pair of snow white stallions
Complete this country scene . . .

GIG

THE SOLDIER ON THE BATTLEFIELD

Out on the battlefield,
A young soldier does stand
Straining to hear over the noise,
The sound of the military band.

Ammunition shells zoom past his head,
As he looks out into the distance,
He thinks of all the ended lives
And all the blood shed.

Armoured vehicles drive past him
Picking up the injured or dead.
They are painted with a cross;
A cross that is red.

Bomber planes drop shells from the sky
Trying to make more people die.
Why do wars have to happen?
Why, oh why?

Soldiers run by with a rifle in one hand,
They don't want to fight
But they are fighting for their country
And their country's land.

But now it's all over.
And the blood has been shed.
The battlefield was once green
But now most of it is stained red.

After the war,
The surviving soldiers
Visit the graves of their friends,
Remembering the moment
In which they met their ends.

Out on the battlefield,
An elderly soldier does stand
Straining to hear above the noise,
The sound of the military band.

Stephen Hunt (14)

ROAD RAGE

They came home yesterday
Now someone is inside
It was their holiday

They always go away
Every Whitsuntide
They came home yesterday

It's only for one day
And just a little ride
It was their holiday

She hates the motorway
he took it in his stride
They came home yesterday

But something went astray
He took a corner wide
It was their holiday

She will survive they say
The hearse is now outside
They came home yesterday

It was their holiday.

James Hodgson

BEHIND CLOSED DOORS

If you visit a house of quarrels
You feel the tension right away
Feel the time was all wrong to come
And don't know what to say

You cannot take sides without the fear
Even when you are asked
Of adding more coal to the fire
And are glad when this visit is past

You pick up the vibes so easily
Wish you were back at home
Unhappy voices fill the air
Here is a state of war zone

If you visit a house of harmony
People living in peace together
Hear the point of view of the other
Any trouble they know how to weather

What a joy to visit such a home
Pass the time with a laugh or two
Knowing that whenever you go there
A welcome is waiting for you

How nice when folk pull together
And reach a compromise
A little bit of give and a little bit of take
And unselfish love as the guide.

Adela Llewellyn

PRECIOUS

And when you wake up,
Everyone will be happy.
Like a life being brought into the world,
When a child speaks their first word.
Miracles that only ever happen once.
When you came into this world,
You brought such a light.
A boy who grew into a man.
A man who grew into somebody special,
So special and very talented,
You have such a gift.
A man who was born to live life to the full,
Which is what you have done,
And will carry on doing.
You are a fighter and will never give up
Without you here many people will feel empty
Many people, including me.

Victoria Sutton

WE CAN ONLY DO SO MUCH

We can only do so much
To help our friends in need
Trying to do our best for them
Their troubles trying to heed

But sometimes we are not enough
To quell their troubled breast
No amount of comfort
Can help them find true rest

They cannot get peace of mind
Turmoil ruins their very life
They are so weighed down with care
Worry, problems strife

We just cannot give to them
The peace they badly need
We must speak to our Heavenly Father
If we are to succeed

In helping them to cope with life
They need the Father's touch
They need to know He's there for them
And loves them very much

They need to know the peace He gives
The calm just by His touch
They need to know they need *Him*
For we can only do so much.

Jean Beardsmore

GEOFF HEMMING IS THE AFTERNOON MAN

Geoff Hemming is
The afternoon
Man
And we
Can
Share our
Tea
With him
Starting at
Three
Then goes around
Seven
To his little
Heaven
For he is in
Charge of our
Radio
So believes in
Doing his own
Show
With all of the
Rest because
Geoff
Is one of the
Best

Coleen Bradshaw

THE BOY WHO STEALS HEARTS

C ongratulations they all cried,
H is parent's joy was hard to hide.
R ight from the start, he stole my heart,
I ronically, he made their world fall apart.
S urgery was the only way,
T o make him last another day.
O pen his heart, make it good,
P lease God, don't let this end my motherhood.
H ooray! Hooray! Our little boy pulled through,
E xcitement and euphoria grew and grew.
R ight from the start, he stole my heart.

P erhaps they knew all along,
E xceptional he did belong.
T oday as he grows stronger,
E veryday's happiness gets longer and longer.
R ight from the start, he stole my heart.

C oping with only one kidney as well,
A h, I've had open heart surgery, so what the hell!
R inging out laughter, screams of fun,
T heir surprise and wonder at how far he's come.
W ith every new day that's here,
R elief and happiness, ebb away the fear.
I ndeed our little man can cope,
G iving everyone some hope.
H e's here to stay, whatever gets in the way,
T hat little boy, who stole my heart.

Michelle J Cartwright

WHO?

Who are the rulers in power?
Who started the flower power?
Who started the scum of trading drugs?
Who infested hotels with bugs?
Who traded a vastly world of gunfire and slugs?
Who named aids and caught it thus?
Who can tell the real truth in us?
Who promises wealth and keeps it from us?
Who is doctor who, and have helped us?
Who is Ford Prefect named as thus?
Who am I, or who are you. Is our destiny
Picked for things just like me or you?
Who is famed for death and stardom, oh yes?

Peter Evans

ON BEHALF OF THEM

The shyness behind your smile
When we first met
Forced into a hello
From mutual friends
Everyone watching
Observing our introduction
On behalf of them
I was speechless
Locked into an everlasting grin
You politely hurried back to your room
I couldn't wait to see you again.

T M Welbourne

MAN AMONG POLLUTED STARS

Travelling on a way to Mars - over
The great universe of stars. Only
Earth below is blue - how our
Generation never cared or knew - such
Virgin sulphurs untouched by hand:
Mighty wonders beyond belief are
Planned. In pride and ignorance we
Live on earth - to destroy all that's
Known since birth. A shooting star
A wondrous crater - an astral
Planet of lateral quator. Sparks
Exploding from the Milky Way - The
Reign of Jupiter we saw today.
All the universe in fact is clean:
Except the place where man has been.

David Hazlett

BIRCHAM RIVER-BED SUNSET

Looking out of my window high and across the fields to
Where you are lovely bright pink, lilac, grey blue sky
Amazement and wonder and I stand and gaze
At your far setting sun, how beautiful you are
Beautiful Bircham river-bed sunset
In wonder I stare, never seen such beauty only you so fair
Towards the twisting narrow roads I roam towards your setting sun
In cold winter's afternoon I hear you cry lovely river-bed sunset
Beside the holly hedge I spy flutter of wings as I pass by
Across the fields I ride on a early winter's night
In the furrows across the sunset for all to see I gallop
Towards your sails Bircham Mill I ride,
In the early evening listening to the wind driving your sails as
                                                                           I gallop by
Faster, faster, no further now I roam
As your lovely pink, lilac, grey blue sky has gone
Gone, disappeared for a while only to return next evening.

Katherine Latham Grimes

MOTHER

The majesty and grace of the lion king
Not afraid of a solitary thing
Carefully watching the wildebeest skyline
As focus and thought unite and entwine
Chasing the gazelle and the antelope
Gliding to the kill with the smoothness of tope
Cubs and mate won't be hungry today
Nature she gives and she taketh away.

D Burke

JUST ANOTHER DAY

Somewhere in the dead of the dry desert
The sand will sink another nuclear bomb
They call it a military testing ground by all accounts
Trying to out manoeuvre nations that are too many for anyone to count
Many would call it a nuclear explosion
But the power men always seem to find words of justification.

A million people are marched across the horizon to their chapel of rest
Their bleeding bodies creating desolate rivers of protest
Politicians and holy peace-keepers vow holy words of never again
Then in disarray tomorrow's papers read to find history repeating itself
Another concentration camp ceasing to exist yet for another generation
And the world's intelligence services in their denials know nothing
A bloody killing field created all over again

Somewhere, some place across the globe in a stretch of land called the Third World
Millions of skeleton children search for a crust of bread and water
Starving in the prolonged sunshine's confusion
When just across the water, mountains of produce is left to rot without
                                       a justifiable reason
Yet not one intellectual mind in the educated world of brain surgeons
                                               and professors
Can figure the simple solution that even the blind can see.

Another day and another remembrance date is commemorated
Another night and another victim's fate is set in concrete
Turn the page and you'll witness the suicide rates increase
Turn the corner and see the terrible crimes we continue to inflict upon
                                               one another
Yet the world continues to spin on its axis
Searching endlessly for a meaning to this cruel creation
Whilst we carry on destroying each other in the name of compassion.

Saheeda Khan

A Night To Remember

Titanic
Man's supreme challenge to the powers of Nature
She was the greatest ship ever known
A steamship, a metal monster
Yet she was like a woman of high society
In fashion
But not necessarily to last

Slicing her way through icy waters that fateful night
Her body gleaming like a silver arrow
She became the jewel of the ocean
Her thousand lights sparkling
Like diamonds on a black, velvet sea

Then, without warning
Death's cold, ironic hand fell

April 14, 1912
A night calm, yet bitterly cold
The 'smell' of the ice was strong, suspicious
A snow-capped mountain
Moving fast like the crater of a volcano
Two mighty warriors, face to face
Yet one had to die

Almost all perished
1513, they wrote in the newspapers
A world in mourning waited upon Carpathia
With her tragic load of widowed wives
And orphaned children

The Tunisian sent a message
Midnight, Saturday, April 14, 1912
'Good Luck Titanic.'

The Titanic replied,
'Many thanks.'

'Goodbye.'

Jennifer Polledri

It Shows In Your Face

You don't have to tell how you live each day,
You don't have to say if you work or play.
A tried and true barometer serves in the place,
However you live, it shows in your face.

The false, the deceit that you wear in your heart
Will not stay inside where it got its start.
For sinew and blood is a thin veil of lace.
However you live, it shows in your face.

If you have battled and won the game of life.
If you feel you've conquered the sorrow and strife,
If you've played the game square and you stand on first base.
You don't have to tell it, it shows in your face.

If your life's been unselfish, for others you live,
And not what you can get but you can give
And you live close to God in his infinite grace
You don't have to tell it, it shows in your face.

William Price

BATH TIME FOR THE DOG

Little Jimmy tried to bath the dog.
Fetched a towel,
Grabbed the mog.
Turned on a tap,
Shoved him in,
Leaned over the bath
Then fell in.
Splashing about water everywhere,
The dog jumped out
With a look of despair.
Jimmy gave chase,
Slipped on the soap.
He's started something,
Now he can't cope.
The dog started shaking and flapping about,
The bathroom's a mess,
Without a doubt.
Bounding down the stairs,
The dog had a fright,
Covered in soap,
What a sight!
Don't know what mum'll think
When she gets home.
Shouldn't have left him
On his own.
With all the commotion
He left on a tap
I'm sorry to say
He's flooded the flat.

Wendy Watkin

THE SAME LANGUAGE

There is no war, the guns have gone,
And there's no one dying of hunger.
Where once corruption ruled the world,
There is distant rain and thunder.

We all speak the same language,
We all see the setting sun
We have learned to feed each other,
Now there's enough for everyone.

But that's a dream, it's not today,
This world is full of sorrow.
We know the hunger of the poor countries,
Yet we'll eat our fill tomorrow.

There are people who walk ten miles a day,
To bathe in the rivers en masse.
And there are others who laze in a bubble bath,
Have champagne from a crystal glass.

If you look around the lands of death,
Where civilians are dying of hunger.
You'll see the generals with their armies at war,
And maybe you'll think, and wonder . . .

Machines of war cost so much,
And the armies are fed very well.
The generals live in palaces,
While civilians are living in hell.

And they call to us to give them aid,
To feed their hungry plight.
Well sometimes I wonder where the money goes!
Does it also feed the fight?

I think this world will always be a divide for rich and poor.
And I think, because there's always greed, there'll always be a war.

Paul Beretta

THE WAY I WISH

Ozone friendly
Pollution free
The way I wish
The world could be
Fresh clean rivers
Deep blue seas
Life infested meadows
Wise old trees
Elephant saved
And the whale swims free
The way I wish
The world could be.

Alan Green

SEASON OF LIFE

Spring pops up from winter
Like the snowdrops arising from their sleep.
The smell of fresh morning dew,
Odd frosty patterns on the windowsill.

Plants have all now rested,
Regeneration has taken place,
Their little batteries charged up from winter
To bloom in the warmth of midday sun.

Birds are all now singing,
Geese are heading back north,
The dawn chorus has new meaning
As to whom will stay or go.

The grasses all seem much greener,
Winter's heavy coats changed for something light,
Hoping and waiting patiently for summer
Till autumn's winds again start to bite.

Michael Chappell

DUMB ANIMALS

Oh no, too placid maybe
The horse that could really maim
Attacked by someone so unscrupulous
But they never get the blame

The dog with those searching eyes
Wonders why on earth it has been kicked

The swan so graceful goes through hell
Some have such awful tales to tell

The elephant so elegant and calm
Have been known to try and bury the
Remains of other elephants
Some coward attacked
The elephant could really have done them harm

Why breed sheep or any animals to send
To suspect countries
Is money so important
We lose our self respect?
And ruin these beautiful lives

The animals could attack
But when they do
The cry goes out

'Put down' the vicious animal
But what made them attack?
Humans are never to blame

Birds in the sky need trees
I am sure the world was not meant for us alone

Maybe that is what happened years before
The animals took over
That would make some coward groan

The whale could have watched and waited
When it saw it was in a similar position
As other whales had been
It knew just what to do

The enemy had struck
Another man intruding

How can this go on?

Phyllis O'Connell

Alone

Shrouded in a mist I do walk alone
trails of deceit lay dormant alongside the skeletons of which
                                              I leave behind
oozing, seeping from my chilled brow fall tears of crimson red
eyes gaunt and hollow
scared in this pitiful hole
no stone unturned
never a disheartening path have I not ventured
deathly predominant eyes pierce through my soul tainted with
                                              pity they stare
I shall descend my aching head no more
for to the soil I do lay shallow in breath empty and cold
I will to sleep
but in peace I cannot

Tammy Louise Gayle Tiffany

LOVE CAME WITHOUT WARNING

In the quietness of early morning
Alone with my dreams,
Memories of you constantly gnawing
Secrets of my heart,
Love that now came without warning.

Knowing intuitively before our talks
You were as imagined
From fleeting encounters on walks,
Wanting to know you
When watching each other like hawks.

At last on entering conversation,
You were that person
Vividly built up in my imagination
Conjured from within,
Eventually becoming a realisation.

From earliest encounters hearts won,
Drawn to one another
Eyes perceived long before reason,
Inner selves revealed,
Everything, except our touch, done.

Reaching the point of consummation
Following awareness,
Gazing into your eyes a revelation,
Blinding inner flash,
As minds and souls joined in elation.

Embracing lovers at last in harmony
Reveals the splendour
Of man and woman in mutual ecstasy,
Each lost in the other,
Uniting in body and spirit uniquely.

Betty Mealand

THE GREED TO HAVE

I looked down at this world of ours,
From high up in the sky,
And thought, 'What am I doing here,
I know that I can't fly.'
All around me, emptiness,
Deep blackness, left and right,
Far down below, our *glowing earth,*
In *greens,* and *blues,* and *white.*
I could see the continents,
In detail, crystal clear
The more I looked, the more I saw
And felt deep inner fear,
Around the earth a halo, blue,
Protective, like a shell,
This thin blue band, our atmosphere,
So fragile, I could tell,
In places it just broke apart,
And left a void, so wide,
Then closed again, as struggling,
Protecting earth, it tried.

Revolving there, below me,
Somehow, suspended here,
The earth just kept on turning,
And now I saw, so clear,
Vast clouds of *black pollution,*
Erupting from the ground,
And then I heard, with terror,
A loud spine chilling sound
The cries of *Starving Children,*
The anguish and the pain,
So many *souls in torment,*
Struggling to regain,
All that was *lost forever,*

Destroyed by man's own greed,
The greed to *have, and have and have,*
Much more than he could need.
Earth's glowing light was fading
As putrid clouds obscured,
The *land,* the *sea,* the i*ce caps,*
No more could be endured.
I felt myself now spinning,
Through blackness, through the night,
Opened my eyes, miraculously,
And saw *dawn's golden light!*

Jim Sargant

My Garden

Looking through my window pane
I watch the darkness creeping down from the sky
The summer breeze blows so gently
To cool the night time air,
The night is here once again
I hear the call of the owl above
I see his eyes so big and bright
He sees a movement close by
He swoops down so fast
To catch his night time feast.
Playing close by the pond
The frogs come out to play
Jumping up and down they go
What is this I hear
Up the path the patter of tiny feet
My friend the fox is here
Looking for his little treat.
How I love my little garden
So full of creatures oh so sweet.

Mary Welsh

BELIEVE

Believe in yourself,
In the power that you have
To control your own life day by day.
Believe in the strength
You possess deep inside,
To guide and enlighten your way.
Believe in *yourself*
As you journey through life,
Your dreams will always come true,
If you follow the voice
Of your soft beating heart,
And *trust,* and *believe* in *you.*

Patricia McDonald

CANDLELIT DINNER

Candlelit dinner, table for two
You loving me, me loving you
The waiter is talking we don't hear a word
When you're in love, nothing is heard
I take your warm hand and put it in mine
Am I in heaven, or simply cloud nine
I look into your eyes of blue
A smile on my face, just for you
You look so lovely, in your low cut gown.
You're my princess, but you haven't a crown
We pick up our glasses and take a few sips
I'm longing to hold you and kiss those soft lips
We rise from the table, we're floating on air
Although there are people, we really don't care
I gently put my arm around your slim waist
And kiss those warm lips, I've been longing to taste
We leave the room, where we sat with each other
It's raining outside and we run for cover
'I love you my darling,' I hold you so tight
'Thank you my angel for a wonderful night.'

B Page

IF ONLY

If only I could run through time
Easily as through the fields
To horizons far and take a glance
At what the future yields.
When I had seen, I'd run straight back
In time to change things, put things right
In time to warn the whole wide world
Of what's beyond their sights.

We could work together, then:
Together we could shape
The future world to our desires,
Not learn when it's too late
Of changes mankind *should* have made
To save our precious lands
And that we *should* have thought about
The future, not just the task in hand . . .

Alas, I cannot run through time,
And nor can any man.
But all of us can think ahead
And look. And change. And plan.

Elizabeth Bulleyment

TO THE NEW-BORN CHILD

As soft as gossamer,
I plant this kiss, and wish, that . . .
I could gather the blush of a rose,
　for your cheeks.
Put your troubles in bubbles, and
　watch them fly.
Gather the gold of sunflowers, to
　colour your hair.
Bless your limbs, so they stay strong.
Touch your heart, so life, is rich
　and long.
Fill your world, with a thousand thrills,
If I had the magic wand of time,
I'd brush away each creeping tear, and
　wash away your smallest fear.
This is my prayer, as I hold you in my arms.

Christine Osborne

LOVE

A wonder, a world of transition
Motivation is every moment
Each thought, as would be, is best intent
So embracing itself in virtue
This aura can know no bound
Even to the extent of self denial.

Born with an ability to challenge
Consume the pressure of outer influence
A consistency of force, pathos
Tranquillity is its symbol: the dove
And in this quality would be unassailable
The state of mood to love.

George

THE WEDDING
(Dedicated to Tracey & Keith Purssord, 8 August 1998)

I give to you
as you give to me
my heart my love
my soul
and with this ring
I do thee wed
and give to you my all

That from this day
until day's end
our love will always be
a union of our hearts entwined
a gift from you to me

Your hand my hand will be our strength
to promise and abide
that though some days may be with rain
our hearts will never hide

Morning has broken
skies are washed with blue
bells toll Jerusalem
I give to you
as you give to me
when we say I do.

James S Jarvis

INCOMPATIBLE

I try hard to like you, I swear that I do.
Yet each time I'm in reach of my goal,
Again without wanting it, back it all comes,
That dislike of you here in my soul.
It's buried too deep,
Sometimes I can't sleep for wondering just what causes me
To suspect you so strongly, even when we agree,
   of cold lack of sincerity.
There's something so sly behind that broad smile,
Your eyes remain watchful in laughter.
Oh no, I don't like you, and you don't like me,
And that's how we'll stay ever after.

Joy Sanders

FOR YOU

She is so beautiful,
everyone loves her.
Her silky soft hair
and the most lovely smile
you're ever likely to see.

She is so kind,
but you won't understand,
you don't know her like I do.

She was my motivation
and my tolerance.
A beautiful flower,
always in bloom.

But then one day,
the wind came
and took her petals away.
The flower stopped growing.

Of course they still lived
but in a new,
much more exciting
place for her.

As the wind blew,
he took her away
to a place
I could never take her.

And I flew away
in another direction
hoping to find another flower
just like her,
but I know I never will.

Julie White

Pain

Beneath the silence
My fears lie
This hell I'm living
Today I cried
I am wounded
But I don't bleed
The scars are there
This I will concede
Enclosed in my world
Hiding from the rain
But inside I'm hurting
That's where you feel the pain

Warren Brown

YOUR EYES

If I never again look deep into your eyes
I will always remember their beauty
They will haunt my dreams for an eternity
I can only remember that long last look
Your eyes holding mine for one moment longer.
How many loves lie behind your eyes.
Silent in your past, never to be revealed.
Woken only occasionally to you in restless dreams.
Is this now my destiny, to become a past love
Lost in the tunnels of your mind
Your eyes spoke silently, no need for words.
Eyes that once looked to mine for love now avoid
My gaze - searching somewhere, unknown to me
Searching maybe for his eyes.
Your words could not speak what your eyes were
Saying. Although with sadness.
Goodbye my love. Goodbye.

Wendy Smith

ANGEL OF THE NORTH

You sprang into my vision
                unawares.
I was looking for you
But when I saw you,
It was with surprise.

A vast impressive figure,
Keeping vigil over all.
A benign but powerful presence,
Rooted and yet hovering.
Still, yet seeming to move.

Taking in all that lies
Behind, around and before.
Like a mother hen
Sheltering her chicks.

So you shield
The northern crowds.
Towering over them,
But not intimidating,
Watching and wakeful.

Guardian Angel of the North.

Margaret Wallis

TINA MY DAUGHTER

Tina my darling daughter is dead
My life now is very dull and sad
Tears for her everyday I shed

Often I suffer alone in my bed
I miss her voice calling me dad
Tina my darling daughter is dead

Compared to the life together we had
I now have nothing to be glad
Tears for her every day I shed

It is as if I have bled
Her death has left me so sad
Tina my darling daughter is dead

My daughter a dear price you did pay
A young life wasted is so sad
Tears for her every day I shed

She has now made her final bed
If in heaven I need not be sad
My darling daughter is dead
Tears for her every day I shed

Albert Moses

THE SANDS OF TIME

Hours wrapped around the seconds,
Weeks around the days.
Our destiny, it beckons,
Floating on the moon's rays.
Lost in this spiral, of moving time,
Gone before you know.
Looking for some kind of sign,
Searching, for that welcoming glow.

Captured in a strange time warp,
Wondering where I'll end?
It ends abruptly, even sharp,
No messages are you able to send.
Cocooned in the minutes,
Cushioned in the hours.
Days to which there are no limits,
Years begin to flower.

Where did everything go?
It had gone, before I knew.
If only I'd known, what to do!
My excuses would have been few.
Now everything's mingled into one,
Seconds, minutes, hours, days.
I wish I'd valued it before it had gone,
But I suppose that's what we all say!

   Value your time as you should
   Grasp it with both hands.
   No use saying, 'If only we could.'
   Because time is like shifting sands.

Gail Susan Halstead

HANDS THAT FEED

Hand over hand
in all weather
hauling winding nets.
Controlled. Strong.

Battling tempest storms
steadying tillers. Firm
often torn, frozen fishy
fingers, gut bellies
sliver throats.

Gesturing gnarled knotted,
shaking old, tall tails
told to all. Wet hooked
nose, back of handcuffs.

Thick fingers stroke
ragged moustache,
reminiscent. Grasping
full cool glass to quaff.

Dorothy Grey

APRIL EVENING

After days, and weeks, of rain, snow, sleet
It enters, such a *sunny* spring filled day
When work done, and evening calls
Then *poets* write of sights and sound that fall.
A gentle warmth is biding, one when souls search,
Words to recall in verse, wise, 'oh they to us revert.'
The setting sun is *etched* by April's own well loved signs around
Those of birds their young feeding or placing head under wing, do sleep
Now a plane leaves a vapour trail, pattern like flock of sheep
These clouds so disturbing, they form pictures true
Daylight dimming a quietness fills the air
Our limbs grow tired, and we too seek sleep.

Jessie F Harper

Swan Song

She keeps herself to herself, they say,
But of course she does - she's had her day
And no-one wants to hear her say,
'When I was young.'-
  The swan's song's sung!

Her hair is now a crown of white
Her face is still a sheer delight
When helping others in their plight.
They say she's just another old crone,
That gracious lady; now old; alone.
Living 'mong people with hearts of stone.

But once she was a pretty girl, with
Golden hair all a curl,
She sent men's hearts all in a whirl -
And in the past, young love did last
A lifetime; It was strong and fast.

So, take heed my friend, don't follow the trend
Of putting the old on the shelf,
It will happen to you, then what will you do,
When you're left alone by yourself?

Ivy Cawood

THE SUPPORTER

Waiting for you to lapse into acute pain.
Can I retain my rock-like stance
Without the cracks showing through?
And when they do
Can we paper over them?

Waiting when you are in hospital for the phone to ring,
To know if they will let you out.
Or if there is still some doubt
And they keep you in.

Waiting, when you are home again,
For you to overdo it in some way
And knowing that you will have to pay
In pain later.

Waiting for us to resume our life together
With always the nagging under-doubt
As to whether
We ever will.

I remember - back fifty five years -
When I was in a fox-hole in Burma.
'Standing-to' for an hour at dusk and dawn.
Time stood still, unborn
Because you knew your life would change
Dramatically at any instant -
You could be killed, maimed, shit-scared or
'Just get a bump in the leg' like me.
But you could not rearrange
One damn thing!

Roy Lewis

KEITH

In autumn 1995, we both lived in Andrew Stewart Hall
At the University of Stirling, a small and lovely campus.
Musician and mathematician, my fellow student Keith
Excels in both these disciplines in his own way.
Fingering a guitar, he wanders a maze of algorithms.

I would knock at his door, and through the steam of a kettle
Boiling for tea, we talked and talked of Doctor Who.
Time enough to forget the mad world outside.
All the time he studies abstract squiggles I cannot understand.
He tells me they will earn him a living. I hope so.

David Tallach

Rust

Unlocking that core door brings its conflict;
hard, for key is rusty, and fragile;
been lost and decaying for decades; clicked,

could bring freedom, or breakage; left sterile
will be forever in its loss orbit.
Turn? Life would never be the same; this stile

could be real, open, truthful; might be lit
to close prison of fear - would be losses -
no hiding - no annihilation. Sit

unknown, to be, in God's Kingdom, a gain
roots re-planted where seed should have been sown
in that deep rich red fertile soil. Regain

all that was lost by turning again? Gone
in again! Dare turn key again; atone?

Robert D Shooter

TO AND FOR OUR BELOVED COUNTRY

Kindness, compassion, vision, justice too
With morals, manners, humour, each to make
A quality which does itself renew
Good neighbours for truth's single meanings sake.
Not freaks of fashion, colours, accents, quirks,
But solid truths without which each one dies
Who at the call of *'doing'* never shirks
Who in the *'being'* reaches for the skies.
A *history* of which we all stay proud
A *literature* the envy of the earth
Science and *manufacture* - (the absurd -
A dash of that!) not captive to the crowd
But in that crowd to honour special worth
And see each *separate citizen* is heard!
Then praise what has been done and what's to do
Standing *'in commonwealth'* to face tomorrow
As what is great makes *active vision* true
And gives a pattern time is prompt to follow.
Service supreme . . . not selfishness unbound
Together in a team which holds one heart
Each *separate* upon a chosen ground
Together in the *life* of *every part*.
Let us not fail by trying to be small
Apologising for *past mighty deeds*
Our *future's* at the dare, we dare not lack
Our *land of hope and glory* stays for all
Cultures and *colours, aims, intentions, creeds,*
The dark confronts *each* . . . *up* . . .*to the attack!*

Jim Hacobian

Upward...

While stars, impassive, gaze from universal height.
We seem beneath their notice on our earthly way.
Yet stars like beacons lead us to the light!

Since time primeval mankind sought the light,
And ever strives and struggles toward the day,
While stars, impassive, gaze from the universal height.

Slow, faltering steps, with upward progress slight,
From depths whence even heaven shies away,
Yet stars like beacons lead us to the light!

More souls determined learn, and grow, and fight,
Our lives to purify, and evil slay,
While stars, impassive, gaze from universal height.

Darkness waxed in purpose and in might,
And always some, despairing, lose their way.
Yet stars like beacons lead us to the light!

Now stand we, voyagers, at the shores of night:
New worlds undreamed of hang in grand array
While stars, impassive, gaze from universal height.
Yet stars like beacons lead us to the light!

Gordon Long

A Photograph

Her porcelain face, her looks, her laugh,
Her flow of soft brown hair . . . kiss, kiss
Her poise her way, her gesturing eye,
Sets hourglass form, and heavenly charm,
And brushes by in glide . . . per chance,
Transfixed my sight, no breath inside,
I sighed, I sighed,
Beautiful bride, beautiful bride,
I wasn't by your side,
I sighed . . .
I wasn't by your side.

Respond my lass, respond my warmth,
Accept my apt for openness,
As a friendly 'Hi' from I . . . kiss, kiss,
In Father's dreams methinks indeed,
To swoon affections from absent friend
Glide by my dear . . . glide by per chance,
No breath inside, my sight transfixed,
I wasn't by your side,
I signed . . .
I wasn't by your side.

Hugh Jackson

AGONY AUNT

'I am writing to you in desperation requesting most sound advice.
My mother's flipped her lid and is frequenting nasty dens of vice.
It's many a year since I visited her, dreaming that all was secure.
She's draining the family fortune so my future reeks like manure.

Having conjured up a toy boy, she's purchasing Saville Row suits!
She flies him to Paris most weekends to strut in high heeled boots.
It's now outlandish fashions from Paris designer outlets she buys.
I fear that he's poisoning her mind as he flashes his admiring eyes.

She used to be oh, so demure, sporting a hundred shades of black.
There was always a bible by her side, no jewels adorned her neck.
Torturing every beaming clergyman around the country for miles,
She showered pennies on their plates, deflating anticipated smiles.

Her wealth was of such repute even the banks sent birthday presents.
Most exceedingly parsimonious she ranked high above the peasants.
I fear that all this has changed with the latest apparition on the scene.
So how should I now council her saving a soul seemingly, so green?'

'Son, it seems to me that you have defaulted by showing great neglect.
If you had carefully looked after her, your fortune would be safe intact!
Left on her own you assumed that she'd rust into a dependable groove.
Your well earned reward is metal fatigue, now try to weld your mood!'

'I've spent many years rolling out advice about the antics of old dears.
Still, I am open to many a fresh surprise concerning their family fears.
Usually potty, they seek to ceremoniously drive all and sundry dotty.
Ought to be filed away as nature's historic bastion of crocodile tears.'

T Burke

EVENING

Evening has arrived,
The sun now awaits its time for setting,
The bird echoes in a distant song.
Darkness covers the earth like a blanket.
Within the stillness and solitude -
As one sits and reflects on the day's events
About to pass by like ships in the night
I bid farewell
Never again to relive that day.

J C Atkinson

PILGRIMAGE

Unremembered seasons come and go
Generations view the same oak tree
Puny in comparison, we build - also destroy, tho'
Possess the power to transcend our brief mortality

If only time retained each finished year
For travelling to the once familiar places.
When safely we roamed, and were happy near
The bustle of concern, their genial faces
Springing from the matrices of memory.
Will the paradise of belief come true
When fate has sealed our destiny
Or time allow the retrogressing rovers through
In a time machine, to their sojourn of dreams?
To living out our span humanity is cast!
Yet, with most of life behind, how appealing seems
That strange procrastination, visiting the past.

Some, eager to begin might blindly leap
Impatient for a shrouding mist to clear . . .
One, awed as a child in a church of marbled sleep
Beyond the faith of innocence, perceiving here
That while mankind remains, hoping for eternity
Aspects of our being successively appear
In certain Immortality

Sheila Manley

PASSCHENDAELE (YPRES 1917)

Passchendaele,
you will remember me into that mud
and a sea that barred my return
but many crosses like me, you should have known,
weren't wondering the reason why.

Passchendaele,
in November I had no more friends,
but only the mud as an icy coat.
The sky was burning in the night on the hopeless crosses
while I was dreaming to go away

But your rain was falling slowly
melting the mud on my tears
- At eighteen the life is a silk thread -
was still singing at daybreak the wind

Passchendaele,
at that daybreak you showed me your blades,
and I saw that they were mud blades:
for many crosses like me, you have already known,
here in the Flanders the absolute king

Passchendaele, you will remember me under that mud
and a mother who was praying my return
The sky was burning in the night on the sleeping crosses
and I couldn't go away any more

But your rain was falling slowly
melting the blood in my tears
- At eighteen the life if a silk thread -
was still singing at daybreak the wind

Passchendaele,
please remember not to burn another sunrise
in that jolly lonely place,
and rest forever
Now sing, sing joyfully
cause the tears have gone
sing, sing loud if you can
and think
that you see the mud
and you see the rain
while you see the words carved in my grave.

Michele Collatina

The Traveller's Faith

When things go wrong, as they sometimes will
When the road you are trudging seems all uphill
When the funds are low, and the debts are high
And you want to smile, but you have to cry
When care is pressing you down a bit
Rest if you must but don't you quit
Life is queer with its twists and turns
As everyone of us sometimes learns
And many a failure turns about
When they might have won had they stuck it out
Don't give up though the pace seems slow
You may succeed with another blow
Success is failure turned inside out
The silver tint of the clouds of doubt
And you never can tell how close you are
It may be near when it seems so far
So stick to the fight, when you are hardest hit
It's when things seem worse, that you must not quit.

Ty Allbright

MOTHER

Mothers are a treasure
And you should give them tender care,
For one day you could turn around
And that treasure's no longer there.
There's no-one in the world quite like her
She's there in good times and bad,
And she is always the person you turn to
When you're feeling sad.
She gives us words of wisdom
That we don't always heed,
But yet she is there to pick us up
When she knows that we won't succeed.
She is the light of your life in childhood.
A shelter from the storm,
A tower that we cling to
In a place that we call home.
So if you still have your mother
Tell her you love her each day,
'Cause you may never get the chance again
If she is taken away.

May Kay

SUBMISSIONS INVITED
SOMETHING FOR EVERYONE

ANCHOR BOOKS '99 - Any subject, light-hearted clean fun, nothing unprintable please.

WOMENSWORDS '99 - Strictly women, have your say the female way!

STRONGWORDS '99 - Warning! Age restriction, must be between 16-24, opinionated and have strong views. (Not for the faint-hearted)

All poems no longer than 30 lines.
Always welcome! No fee!
Cash Prizes to be won!

Mark your envelope (eg *Poetry Now)* **'99**
Send to:
Forward Press Ltd
1-2 Wainman Road, Woodston,
Peterborough, PE2 7BU

OVER £10,000 POETRY PRIZES TO BE WON!

Judging will take place in October 1998